I0072824

Food People Management

by

Shawn Bucher MBA, CEC, CCE, CCP

Want to learn more about the author and this publication?
http://www.businesschef.org

Original Copyright 2019, Shawn Bucher DBA First Timer's Enterprises, Inc.

All Rights Reserved.

No part of this may be reproduced, copied or otherwise used without the express written consent of the author or publisher-Business Chef Publishing.

ISBN: 9 780578 507095

Library of Congress Cataloging-in-Publication Data: Pending

Food People Management / Shawn Bucher

Food People Management

By

Chef Shawn Bucher, MBA, CEC, CCE

Table of Contents

Introduction

About the Author

Prologue: The Spice Rack: A culinary coaches manifesto to cooks everywhere.

Introduction

Common sense is not so common. At least nowadays for those of us who live and work in kitchens and food service. Tasks and directions given to our staff that seem-to us-to be fairly straightforward and easily understood, unfortunately are not. This begs the question, has it always been this way?

When I got into this industry almost 25 years ago it was kind of like the Wizard of Oz. No one really cared what was behind the curtain. Not many people were really that interested in how the food got out or how pretty it was, just that it got out and was least slightly appetizing. People did not have the same fanaticism that they do today about where the food came from, how it was prepared and who prepared it. It was just different.

In the mid 1990's we went through a food revolution, which had a lot to do with the advent and creation of the Food Network. All of the sudden food and cooking became much more interesting, much more attractive, much more accessible and much more real.

In the decades following this, a kind of natural evolution occurred from this new found food interest. Culinary schools and cooking classes began to open rampantly across the country. Food bloggers and review sites became a major part of the food industry. Chef's became rock stars.

No longer did a chef hide in the kitchen, they became celebrities and reality TV stars. They licensed their names and brands and sold cookware. They taught exciting cooking classes to live studio audiences and had their own catch phrases. They moved away from classical French cooking methods and recipes to into modern science and art. How food was plated and presented became almost more important as how it tasted and smelled.

   Today, we take pictures of everything we eat and share it across social media and other mediums. We have all become much more educated and aware of our food. Documentaries, reality shows and opportunities to write or talk about food as an expert (self-proclaimed or otherwise) have become part of our culture. And with that shift in thinking, came a shift in the food industry as well.

Sometimes when change happens or things evolve there are unintended consequences of things happening the way that they do. When it comes to the food industry, the evolution to where we are today is such a good thing in many ways. We have been able to move toward more sustainably producing food. We have seen a rising in the level of understanding and education among patrons that has required us as chefs and operators to increase our skills and educations to rise to the occasion. Our food is better than it has been in the past, because our customers understand it, and they demand it.

Unfortunately the negative effects are more pronounced as well. The biggest challenge facing us as operators today, aside from the ongoing challenges of controlling costs, rising food and energy costs, an increasingly volatile political climate, etc. Is the labor pool from which we draw.

Increased education is good thing and increased expectations are not bad, but unrealistic expectations are. What do I mean by this? Well, take a step into my world for a moment and let me explain.

In 2009 I began teaching culinary school for a national organization that was owned by a large parent corporation that owned and operated multiple private for-profit institutions, the largest of which I taught for. After a year of teaching I became aware that these private for-profit institutions had come under scrutiny for taking federal student loan dollars that they did not qualify for. An institution could not pay recruiters incentives to recruit students to come to school and take federal student loan money. Although our organization said that they did not do that, an undercover government investigation proved otherwise. I myself witnessed firsthand some of the outright lies that students were told by recruiters to get them to enroll in the college that was incredibly overpriced and had less than stellar results for the students graduating. Don't get me wrong, I believe that students are ultimately responsible for their own success or failure, but this institution was not setting them up to succeed. It was setting them up for a lifetime of student loan debt, with not enough earning power to justify the cost. It was setting them to live a very difficult cash-strapped life-in an already difficult business.

After the federal government announced that it would be suing the parent company of our institution to the tune of 5 billion dollars, I began to feel that I was guilty by association (even though I was able to walk away with my integrity 100% intact) and I just knew that I could not continue on in my role as an instructor for this institution. It was after one particular meeting in which we as instructors were told that we had to do whatever we had to do to get students to stay, or *we* would be let go, that I decided the grass was greener elsewhere and I hit the road-literally. This would signal the official start to my traveling and consulting career...But I digress...

The students that came to this institution seeking a culinary school education did get an education and many of them did get a degree. Many of them have stayed in touch with me and many of them are still in the industry and are doing well. But most of them, never finished and didn't stay in the industry.

As with anything, you get out what you put in. Many of the students who were there realized that a career that rewards experience and loyalty more than degrees and awards, wasn't for them. They realized that coming out of school with no experience and a degree was only going to get them from starting at $8 an hour to maybe $10 and hour. Most were smart enough to see that paying off $60,000 to $100,000 in student loan debt while trying to live on $10 an hour wasn't going to cut it.

But many were lead to believe that the sky was the limit and that a degree from this institution was going to give them an edge. They were told that if they wanted to have a show on the Food Network they could have one. They believed that they would walk out of the school, diploma in hand, into an executive chef role making $80,000 a year and working 40 hours a week. Now, for those of us who have grown up I this industry, we know that this is not the reality of our business. That is what I mean by unrealistic expectations. They are dangerous and can cause unintended consequences.

Although this school example is just my experience, it is happening in many ways to many people looking to make a career in food service. They see the glamour and glitz of celebrity chefs and media personalities and think that in just a few short years they can have their own string of restaurants too.

But the reality of this, is that it's not reality. We live in a food service world that is hot, fast, demanding, dirty and thankless-most of the time. Food service is not a well-choreographed cooking class that consists of all of your ingredients perfectly prepared and laid out in little containers before you. It's too often the most difficult of circumstances involving a mix of late deliveries, broken equipment and unreliable employees.

Anthony Bourdain was telling the truth...

Now, most of us understand that the settings aren't always the same and that the pace is not always as grueling as we make it out to be-but it is difficult. I have always said that if you can make it in the food service world you can make it anywhere. In what other business do you have to manage manufacturing, human resources, retail operations, maintenance and high stress deadlines all day long-everyday!?

So why does anyone want to work in this nut-job of a career? Well, for anyone who's been in it for a while and chooses to stay, we know that it gets in our blood and we can't shake it. We live off the adrenaline highs of just nailing it during a busy rush. We live off of the passion that we have for creating, executing and delivering a product and service that is both never-endingly trendy and life sustaining.

Food is truly and undying industry, people will always want to eat. So at least we have that going for us.

But what about the people who work in this industry, not because they are passionate about it, but because they have no other choice. Even though working in food service has gotten a better reputation over the years, it is still an entry level industry that employs more people than almost any other industry. We are kidding ourselves if we believe that everyone who works in food wants to be doing what they are doing. Many of our peers are here because they have to be, not because they want to be.

This book is for those of us who manage food people...We are a different breed.

Whether it's fast food, fine dining, large institutional (university, hospital, etc.) feeding, grocery stores, casual dining, gas/convenience stores and everyone in between, the strategies and thoughts contained herein are based on my two plus decades of managing those who both want to be working the industry and those who feel they have to work in the industry. This is stuff is tried, tested and proven to work.

My hope it that this book will help those of us who have chosen to make this industry our careers, manage more effectively.

Manage those who see food service as a either a jail sentence or as a short-time stepping stone to something better, as well as managing those who love it, are invested in it and have the same passion for it that we do.

The principles in this book are universal and can be applied to other industries outside of food service as well. So if you decide that this industry just isn't for you... The good news is, at least you're not wasting your time by reading this and utilizing these principles.

<u>Chapter #1</u>

Your Food Service Family

We spend a lot of time at work. That is the nature of this business and there isn't a whole lot of ways around it. No one gets into the food service world to take it easy or because they want to spend more time at home. A lot of us would like to get out of this never ending cycle and no matter what segment of the industry we work in, we would all like a better work/life balance.

So instead of trying to find ways of getting out of working and spending time at work, we can simply acknowledge that is the case and work through it. We take the time off when we can and hope that things work out when we aren't there. Easier said than done, right?

To most of us the thought of leaving "the kids" is a scary thought. That's why when we walk out those doors we can't simply disconnect completely, regardless of how our minds, our spouses, partners, family members, friends and significant others beg us to. It's the *Catch 22* double-edged sword. We wonder and worry if we don't hear from anyone while we are gone how things are going and why we aren't hearing anything. But then, when people do call us, our heart rate increases and our eyes role even before we answer the phone.

So is that just how things are? Are we to doomed to be kept in this perpetual conundrum of wanting to know what is going on but hoping that no one calls to tell us?

The answer I found to this lies in how we view our coworkers and counterparts. Years ago when I first go into management I felt that no one could do things quite the way that I could. I found that things just really went a lot better when I was there running the show.

The problem was, that wasn't reality. That was my perception, which in turn was my reality. But that wasn't everyone else's perception or reality. The people I worked with and lead did not share my sentiments of having to always be there or the place was going to burn down. A few months into my first management job I received this wake-up call, loud and clear.

I worked at night, swing shift, 2pm to midnight. I oversaw multiple food service outlets in a hotel setting. It was a big job for a guy that had never done a job like that before. But after some practice, I was good at it because I worked my guts out. I was good at it because I spent a lot of time in each one of the outlets and never sat in the office (unless it was after the rush was done and I needed to place orders or get a schedule out). My whole process was reactive and I spent some much time running myself into the ground both mentally and physically.

Things changed one holiday season as the banquets were too numerous and business in each one of the outlets was so overwhelming that I simply couldn't get everywhere I needed to be. At the end of one of the busier evenings I collapsed in my chair in the office around 11pm and just kind of stared off into space, wondering if this was what my life was going to be for the foreseeable future. The thoughts of becoming an accountant and working 9 to 5 with holidays off became more and more prevalent as my body and mind sank into a sleep-depraved depressed state. My legs becoming Jello-like and my headache increased from lack of water and stress. As I put my head down on the desk, it could not have been there for more than 2 minutes before I heard one of my line cooks come by the door on the way out to the back dock. I heard the footsteps stop and I looked up slightly to see who was there to gander upon my demise.

"Hey Chef, you ok?"

His hands holding onto the door frame as he pushed himself from side to side and shifted his weight from foot to foot. A very common survival practice for anyone who has ever had to work long hours on their feet. Keep moving, always keep moving so that pains and aches in your legs and feet can't catch up.

"Yeah… Just beat." I said as I sat up and slouched back into the chair.

"You want me to lock up the walk-ins tonight so you can go home?"

Now some of you might think this is ridiculous, but that statement was such a game changing question for me. Up till this point I had never even thought about giving up some of my responsibilities to other very capable folks. Until this point I had never even considered not locking up the walk-in doors before I walked out. But the second he asked me this, my whole world changed. The way I thought about my job, managing, leading and the relationship of managers and staff got turned on its head.

I realized that I could empower people I worked with to take on additional responsibilities so that I could then in turn have more time to be a more effective manager. Or better yet, in this instance, go home a little early.

But the most important lesson I learned that night was that I was not alone and that we were all in this together. And that as each one of us did our job, it made everyone else's job that much easier. Yes I was a manager and yes I had some additional responsibilities from other employees, but I began to see us all as equals. I began imagine and see the possibility of a symbiotic system that was the Food and Beverage department.

I realized that without the store room clerks there to receive and put away the orders, the prep cooks would have nothing to prep. I began to see that the prep cooks made the line cooks who they were. Without items pre-pared and ready to assemble on the line, the line cooks could not accom-plish those incredible ticket times and cook those beautiful dishes. I saw the service staff of waiters and waitresses in a totally different light. With-out their dedication to serving our guests, that food would never get to them in the way that it should. And without the bussers and dish crew, the line cooks and servers would have nothing to put food on, no canvas to paint the creations that our guests were paying for.

As this understanding came upon me, so did the realization that we were a family. Going forward as I watched this symphony of systems and players come together each night I saw everyone as individuals. Individual human beings with problems, concerns, hopes, dreams and aspirations. Human beings just like me that wanted to show up each day and be proud of what they did, get paid for it and go home feeling good about their efforts. They didn't need a tyrant or dictator directing them, they needed a leader. Someone who knew the challenges and struggles that they faced each day and helped make their job easier, not harder.

I had to be the kind of person that I wanted to be led by. I had to be patient and understanding, but firm, just and consistent. I had to be true to my word and practice what I preached. I couldn't ask them to do something that I myself was not willing to do. I had to be willing to admit when I was wrong, and make hard decisions when called to do so.

So it is with all of us. We all want to be led by people that we respect and empower us. We want to be treated fairly by leaders who act with integrity and do what they say they are going to do, when they say they are going to do it.

That's why when we see our employees and staff members as other human beings with personal lives, we can better empathize with them and do what it takes to make them effective in their jobs.

We spend just as much, if not more time, with our coworkers as we do our family. It's important that we treat them as such.

Chapter #2

Servant Leadership

When we lead by example with patience, humility and confidence, we will more quickly gain the trust and confidence of our team members.

As leaders and fellow family members, we should never be above doing anything that needs to be done. When the going gets tough, we shouldn't just assume we know what is best and jump in and bail people out, without truly accessing where we can be the most effective.

This was a hard lesson for me to learn. I remember thinking, "I'm the leader so I should be the best at every job." So when rushes happened, I figured I always had to jump into the busiest spot and just take over. After doing this a few dozen times, I realized that this couldn't be the best way. So instead of coming to the line and just kicking people out of their spots and taking over, I simply started asking, "What do you need me to do?"

If they needed me to jump in I would, but a lot of times they would just ask me to expedite, or take out an overflowing garbage can, or get more plates, etc.

I found that by humbling myself and becoming their servant, I was essentially being the best leader that I could be in that moment. I was supporting and assisting them, we were all getting our jobs done effectively and our guests were being taken of well. Servant Leadership – serving those you lead by supporting them in whatever way is needed at that time. This became my mantra.

This doesn't mean that you let people take advantage of you or walk all over you. Or that you just do the parts of every one's job that they don't want to do. It means that when the need arises and you have the ability, you help however you can. This will make you part of the team and garner the respect and trust of your fellow team members. You will have to step in a take charge at times too, but only after you assess the situation and determine that is what is best. People are more likely to follow you when they know you care, you're a team player and that you practice what you preach.

Chapter #3

The importance of Communication & Educating

Notice how I said educating and didn't say education. Most people get confused by the term education in this context, thinking that I'm referring to diplomas and degrees. What I'm referring to when I say educating is the importance of explaining the "why" behind doing something, as well as the how to do it, or the way in which we want it done.

People are always more likely to do something when they understand why they are doing it. Not just because they have been told to do so.

You see, as food service managers, we want get caught up in a lot of putting out the daily fires and acting *reactively*. Someone comes to us with an issue and we are there to solve it. Because most of the time, the issues that arrive are not issues that can wait.

"The walk-in isn't working."

"(Insert name) didn't show up and lunch starts in 30 minutes."

"(Insert name) has to leave because (insert emergency) and I can't get a hold of anyone to cover."

"The health department just walked in."

"The delivery truck is late and I need (insert item) to start."

etc. etc. etc.

So even if we are *proactive* and plan out our day, we usually get knocked off course early on and then spend the majority of the rest of our day just playing catch up. This is what I mean by being reactive versus proactive. The reality of this business and the nature of being a food service manager is that we will be reactive more than proactive. The question is, how do we acknowledge this, but still work around it? We can't just continually be reactive and throw our hands up in the air and say, "well, that's just how it is." We need to be proactive and create systems that allow us to step back from the front lines of putting out the fires and get above the chaos to create plans for forging ahead.

The first step in doing this is by having a vision of what we want our restaurant, our department or our facility to look like and then work toward that by working backwards from it.

Let me say that in real life everyday operation terms...

We know what we want, and we create a way for our team to get there.

Chapter 4

Mindset & Vision

Your mindset will determine not only how you view the world, but how you view your other team members.

Let's look at how it works...

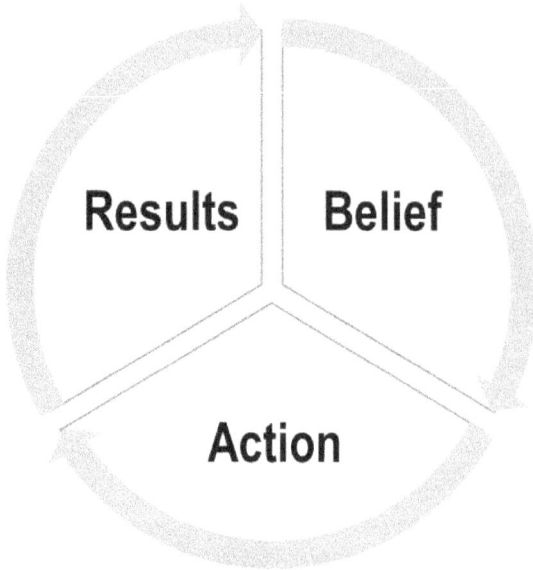

Belief is essential. You must first believe that something can happen or is even possible. If you believe in something, that will drive you to do something about it.

Action. Nothing happens unless you take action. But if we don't believe that something can happen or if we think it has very little potential, then we won't end up taking any action. But if we believe something can happen, then take action, we will see...

Results. Once we take action and see results, we are much more likely to believe that it can happen or that the process works. Seeing results, helps us to believe more-and therefore take more action.

It's our job to help our team members recognize this process and see that we need to believe and take action so we can see results.

Having a vision is crucial, but most food service managers have very little in the way of knowing how to come up with a vision or even what having a vision really is.

When asked what their vision is, I have found that most first time managers (and some long time managers) will give you the "how" to accomplish their vision, not "what" their vision actually is. For example, I recently asked a former culinary student of mine (who now manages a department for one of my consulting clients) what her vision for her department is. She began to tell me that it was going to be clean, the grab-and-go cases would be kept full and the staff would be productive and happy and not want to leave. While all those things are great, that is more of a "how" than a "what." Your vision should be one, two sentences, max. It should be similar to a goal in nature. If we stick with our example above, the vision would be something like "To be the highest performing department in the store." The how would be to keep things clean, keep the grab-and-go cases consistently full and keeping staff happy.

To take this to higher level, you could be even more specific by saying your vision is to be "The cleanest, highest grossing, most sought after department to work in."

Goals are similar, but goals should be more SMART (Specific, Measurable, Attainable, Realistic, Timely or have a time period associated with them) in nature, whereas a vision can be slightly more abstract and far reaching.

Having a vision is important because it gives you a goal and something to shoot for. It gives you more purpose and direction and keep you on track, especially when making decisions. You are more likely to make decisions that will move you closer to your vision if you know what your goal/vision is. Chances are you will probably make different decisions than maybe you normally would because you can constantly ask yourself if the decisions you are making are helping you get closer to your vision, or not.

Once you have a vision of what you want, you need to be able to communicate that vision to your team, get them to buy into it (collaborating with your team to come up with what you want your vision to be is a great way to get buy in) and then create a pathway to all get there.

What does this process look like?

Try this exercise:

1. Sit down with your team and educate them first about what a vision is.

2. Share with them your vision.

3. Ask them their opinions on the vision. Do they see things similarly? Do they have ideas on how it might be different? The optimal situation is to make them apart of the discussion and create a vision together.

People are much more likely to buy into a vision or goal if they have had a hand in creating it. They will be much more invested from beginning to end (as well as on an ongoing basis) if their input has been considered and they feel heard and valued.

Chapter 5

(Standards + Accountability) Consistency

= Success

Before we jump into this, it's important to keep in mind that everything is relative. What I mean is that what is obvious to me, may not be obvious to you.

Everyone has different experiences and perspectives that are shaped by our beliefs and experiences. So before we look at something as "common knowledge" we need to keep in mind who we are talking to and their understanding and perspective. For example, if I am talking to someone about traveling and getting on airplanes and how tight the seats are, I assume that they have been on an airplane and can relate. But if that person has never been on an airplane, they really don't have much of an understanding of what I'm talking about because they have never experienced it the way I have.

This happens every day in our establishments in different ways. We might tell our staff that we want the floors clean, which in our minds mean to sweep and mop and have not debris present. To our staff that could simply mean that there is no debris present, but not mopped.

That's why when we create our standards, we have to effectively communicate what EXACTLY they are and EXACTLY how we get them accomplished.

(Standards + Accountability) Consistency

= Success

(Standards + Accountability) Consistency = Success

Setting Standards can be a daunting task because of the level of thought and detail that goes into to. We have to be open to the possibility that the way we want it done may not be the best way. That's why when setting standards I believe that it should be a collaborative effort. Not collaborative between you and the other members of the management team, but collaborative between you and your entire team.

The people who work in the jobs and positions every day that we are setting standards for have tremendous insights into the best way to get things done. Now, with that said, it's important to note that even though you are asking for feedback, you still have the ultimate say in what the final resolution is. The employees that we seek feedback from should be able to give that feedback in an open and honest way without fear. We should be open to their opinions and insights and look at everything objectively. Even if we have told them to do something a particular way, if that way is not working or does not work as well as something else, we need not take what they are telling us as a personal attack, simply as a possible alternative. Just two (or more) adults have a conversation about how best to run the operations for the betterment of the entire organization.

This is probably the best way in which you can gain credibility and trust with your team as well. The old saying that people "don't care how much you know, till they know how much you care" applies here. People are much more apt to "buy-in" to an idea or concept if they have been a part of the decision making process. If they understand why they are doing something and how the decision for them to do something a certain way came to be, they are much more likely to do it. Especially if they were part of that decision making process. This helps people feel like their opinions truly matter and that they are a part of the team. Plus, you gain the trust of your team when you say you're going to do something and then actually do it. It's just an all-around great way of doing business that makes your job easier and endears your team to you more completely.

Once we gain all of the information from our counterparts (employees and fellow management team members) then we can look at the pros and cons of each person's perspective and determine what the best course of action is. You have the final decision, therefore, make a decision and move forward. Too often I see managers crippled by the idea of making a decision. They spend so much time asking for opinions and feedback that they forget to actually make a decision. The longer it takes you to make a decision and move forward, the less credibility you have with your staff. If people see you as indecisive they are much less likely to bring you ideas or suggestions because (from their perspective) "what's the use? It's not like anything is going to happen..."

Setting Standards

Create a system for setting standards and getting feedback. If you do, you will have standards in place before you know it. If you don't, it will take you forever to get anything accomplished and it will become a burden and something that you put off and dread doing.

Here is what I like to do when it comes to setting standards.

First, I identify issues in the establishment that need a standard. For example, who takes the garbage out, how do they do it and how often do they do it? Now, some of you are saying, "well that sounds like something that should just go into some one's job flow and then I can forget about it." If that's you, then refer back to what I talked about being a family and everyone working toward a common goal. Everyone should know how to do things like taking the garbage out. This is something that anyone should be able to do, and something that anyone can do in times where help is needed. You might not be able to jump in on the line and do things that require practice and skill like cooking eggs or steaks, but when the cooks need help on the line and one of the things that will help them is by getting the overflowing trash taken out, or buss tubs emptied or more product brought to the line, etc. Everyone should know how to do this so that anyone and everyone can help out at a moment's notice.

Once we have identified what items need a standard, we need to make sure that what we are seeing is what our team is seeing too.

Second, get feedback from your team (continuing along the same lines of what we just discussed using our garbage example). We need to huddle with our team and let them know that one of the things we have noticed that needs to be addressed is how the garbage is taken out. If the team agrees, then we move forward with discussing a solution. If they mention that they think there is no problem there, discover why. They may have a system in place already that you simply don't know about. By finding this out and simply documenting the procedure so that there is no confusion for future managers, you gain credibility from your team. Because you truly are working on things to make their life better, and they see it, they will be much more likely to share and be forthwith in the future for other discussions. If they think that you're just doing things for the sake of doing them rather than focusing on the areas that the team feels they need the most help, they will be withdrawn or silent.

Third, take the feedback and create a policy, procedure or otherwise documented standard (depending on where you work you may call it something different but whatever you call it, it's a standard to hold people accountable to). This should be done in such a way that it communicates effectively, meaning that anyone who reads or looks at it will be able to understand how to it.

Once you have created a standard, you're only half way there. The next step is probably the most important part of implementing standards.

Fourth, communicate and train your team on the standards. Without doing this, you won't be nearly effective as you could be. You might as well just do what most people do and post a bunch of paper all over your walls and expect people to follow it. Sure, maybe you might tell them about what the paper says, but they won't internalize it and it will become just another piece of wall clutter that is forgotten just as fast as it was posted. Communicating and training takes time and effort.

That's why most people don't do it. It's a lot easier just to send an email and post yet another piece of paper on the wall than it is to spend time with people making sure they understand why they are doing something and how to accomplish it.

The kind of communication I'm talking about is not just telling someone something. It's explaining something to them so completely that they can then explain it back you in a way that lets you know they understand it. The same goes for training. They must be able to replicate the actions you are asking them to perform in a way that was as if you were doing it yourself each time.

We all learn in different ways. Some of us learn by someone telling us, others learn by seeing it done and others have to actually do it to comprehend what is being asked of them.

To get to this level of understanding for all the different learning types you must spend time explaining, showing and doing the actions that you are asking them to perform. Then having them repeat the actions so that you know they understand.

> *Explain* what it is you would like them to do so that there is no way that they can misunderstand.
> *Show* them what it is that you would like them to do, so that the visual learners will understand more completely.
> *Teach* the teacher or train the trainer (the phrase that many organizations use).

Making it Happen

So let's bring this all together now. To explain this whole process to the reader more thoroughly, let's go back to our garbage example.

If I was to set the standard for taking out the garbage, I would first recognize that a standard needed to be set for taking the garbage out. This might be because I observed inconsistencies in how my team was doing it, or maybe I observed a problem in how it was being done… or not done.

Next I would go to my team and tell them that I believe that a standard/policy/procedure needed to be set for taking out the garbage. I would then ask for their feedback and insights. After getting their input, I would proceed to document a way in which we wanted to accomplish this. After I created a document detailing how we were going to do it, I would then present that to my team again and make sure that it is what we had agreed upon.

After this, I would explain the document to my team and reiterate the reason(s) why we were creating the standard. I would then physically show them how we would like it done. After showing them how we wanted it done, I would then have one or more individuals demonstrate exactly what I had just shown them.

The greatest part of this is that, once you use an employee to model this behavior, they can then own it. So if by chance you have other things going on (which you almost always will) you can then call on that employee to show the new employee or retrain the employee who has maybe "forgotten" what they were originally shown. This is one of the ways in which you can hold others accountable to the standards set as well.

(Standards + **Accountability**) Consistency

= Success

(Standards + **Accountability**) Consistency = Success

Setting standards is one of the most time consuming parts of either opening a food service establishment or taking over an existing place. This is one of the reasons why the franchise model works so well for food businesses. The time that it takes to initially create the standards is significantly decreased-because they have already been figured out, tested, adjusted again and again until they are solidified.

If setting the standards is the initial challenge, then accountability is the ongoing challenge. That is why there will always be a need for managers, someone will always need to be the one that enforces standards and hold people accountable to those standards. Human nature is such that we will always try to take the path of least resistance. If there is a way that is easier, less stressful or quicker, we will default to that. Understanding this not only helps us to stay on top of keeping people accountable, but it helps us create standards that will ultimately be easier to hold people accountable too. We want to make our jobs easier, so why create standards that are too hard to enforce and hold people accountable to?

How to hold others accountable

Most of how we hold people accountable to standards is first have a standard and then make sure that everyone understands it and then hold them accountable to following it.

That's why many times people are required to sign a document that they have been shown how to do something. So that when we ask why a standard isn't being followed the never ending excuse of "I didn't know," or "no one ever showed me," doesn't hold any weight. We can then refer them back to their signature or acknowledgement verifying that indeed they did know, and simply did not follow through on it like they said they would.

Now, if they say that didn't understand it, this could be something that usually needs to be addressed one-on-one. There might be some learning issues such as illiteracy and possibly dyslexia or other learning disabilities that will require some additional support. A lot of times these issues do not surface until after something happens where they are not able to cover up their challenge. That is another reason why by showing someone how to do something in addition to telling them how to do it, you can overcome these challenges before they become issues. Unfortunately most people do not want to readily admit that they have a learning disability or other challenge. It's important to be empathetic to these challenges and try to accommodate them as best as possible, if the employee is willing to work with you, you should be willing to work with them to create a compromise.

If they are unwilling to work with you, you may have to make some hard decisions as to whether not that employee needs to move into a different more suitable position or move on somewhere else altogether. This is a hard thing for us to learn as managers when we see our teams as our families and close associates. But if we don't make hard decisions, then a few bad grapes can in-fact spoil the whole bunch.

An associate of mine named Carlton Green, was an award winning food service director for many years and is known widely throughout the healthcare food service industry. He was responsible for a major turnaround of a very large property in southern California that had many challenges. Carlton had the perfect way of expressing letting people go. He would say that it is our job (in this context of holding people accountable) to "set people free." What he means by that is, if our employees do not want to play by the rules and be a part of the team and abide by the standards, we do not want (or have time) to force them to do so. We are actually doing them a favor by setting them free to go find an opportunity where they will be more comfortable and happy. As managers and leaders it's not our job to change anyone. All we can do is simply provide an environment in which people can thrive-if *they* choose to do so. If someone chooses to not thrive with us, we can set them free to thrive elsewhere in an environment more suitable for them.

It might be hard to do, but the best managers are able to stay objective when it comes to discipline. They keep it about the act or mistake. That way it's not about the person, only about the circumstance. By addressing the fact that a standard was communicated and agreed to, but then not lived up to, it's not personal. It's factual and objective. A good employee will see it similarly and not hate their employer/manager/leader for doing their job and holding them accountable. It is what it is. If you, as a manager, can separate out the emotion and stay objective, both parties will be better off for it. It's never comfortable having to hold people accountable, but it is absolutely necessary and there is no faster way to either gain or lose credibility with your staff.

Part of accountability is making sure that the initial training is done thoroughly. Assuming that the training and communication have been done effectively, then we should live by the 3 strike rule...

Strike 1 – Verbal Warning – We let the person in question know that they have not lived up to our standards. This is best done in a private setting. The old saying of "praise in public, discipline in private" is applicable. Some human resource departments require this step to be documented and I would encourage you to do so. It's very important to document any disciplinary conversation had with anyone, especially in our overly-litigious society. This can be done as simply as sending an email or actually writing a detailed account of the conversation. However you do it, make sure you note the date and time that the conversation and any action plans and timelines that need to be accomplished by either party. In other words, write down the date and time you talked to them and what you asked them to do about correcting the behavior. Let them know that if they don't comply what the next steps are.

Strike 2 – Written Warning – If again they fail to meet the standard set, this becomes their last chance to do so. A written warning is very similar to a verbal warning, but now, when you document it, both parties see the document and sign it-signifying that both parties acknowledge the circumstance and possible repercussions should the behavior/acts/misdeeds, etc. continue.

Strike 3 – You're out – If an employee or team member fails to take it seriously or they fail to comply with the first two warnings then you have no choice but to terminate their employment and "set them free."

This last step is easier said than done, especially in big beau acratic organizations. And even more especially if unions are involved. If you are working in these types of situations then you will have to comply with whatever the-powers-that-be tell you to do. This can be incredibly frustrating, but the key is diligence and persistence in these scenarios. Many employees learn the rules of the system and then work that system. Again, it is what it is. Just stay the course and eventually things will work out, regardless of however long or frustrating the circumstances maybe.

Other lessons that managers must learn when it comes to keeping our teams accountable...

Trust but Verify

Although we want to trust our people and we want to believe that they are always doing what they need to be doing, when they need to be doing it, that just isn't always the reality.

We don't think they are stealing, but we still need to put controls in place so someone won't. We don't think they would ever lie to us, but when they do, we hold them accountable.

Generally speaking, only those who have something to hide will be overly defensive if they are ever called out for something. If you have nothing to hide and you are doing what you're supposed to, you are fine with someone asking you about where the missing money went or where you actually were that day you called out sick. Because you really didn't take the money and you really were at home sick. You're not out of line as a manager for calling someone in and asking them questions if something doesn't add up. You're simply asking questions. You trust them, you're simply verifying.

Don't Bless Bad Behavior

What do I mean by this? Because we are so busy, we often rush here and there and pass through prep and service areas and past employees working without stopping. When we do stop we most certainly will see things that are out of line with the standards we have put into place.

For example, we might require fruits and vegetables be washed before they get prepared. So as we are walking through the kitchen we notice that this isn't happening, the prep cook(s) are simply taking them out of the box and preparing them. But because we are in too much of a hurry we think "I'll address this with them later" or "I need to talk to the supervisors about this." So instead of addressing this, we simply walk on or briefly acknowledge the employee with something like "Hi, (insert name), how are you?" and we hurry on.

The problem with this is that the prep cook(s) notice, if just subconsciously, that they weren't washing the produce and YOU didn't say anything. Which means that they might be able to skip this step in the future also. All of the sudden their job just got easier and human nature dictates that we default to the path of least resistance.

You could use this example for most any task, especially the ones that require extra effort and might seem not all that important to our front line staff. Taking temperatures, changing out utensils and pans, breaking down boxes, cleaning before they go on a break, getting new sanitizer buckets or any other task that we have to continually remind people to do.

The problem with not saying anything is that people will try to get away with it if they know we won't say anything. We give our "blessing" to bad behavior when we walk past it. But once our staff knows we are going to say something EVERY time we see it, they are much more likely to do it without us asking. No one likes to be badgered or reminded, so the more we do it, the more likely they will do everything without us even asking.

(Standards + Accountability) **Consistency**

= Success

(Standards + Accountability) **Consistency** = Success

The most difficult part of what we do every day is to be consistent. That's why the equation is Standards plus Accountability *times* Consistency. The more *times* we hold people accountable to the standards the more effective and successful we become.

It is hard to keep emotion out of what we do because by nature food people are passionate people. We stay in this business because we love serving ... or creating ... or the pace and excitement ... or a myriad of other reasons. We love what we do, we are passionate about it and we sacrifice a lot to be able to do it for a living.

Being able to sometimes contain that passion during a busy rush when something goes wrong or when someone doesn't share our passion and commitment can let the emotional door open. And usually what comes out is not always ideal. Nowadays, being consistent is not only necessary it is expected from every level of the hierarchal food chain. If we don't want our boss yelling or taking their frustrations out on us, we can't take our frustrations out on our team members. If we don't want our managers to act rashly and make our team members feel belittled or intimidated then we can't act in that way either. We are servant leaders, we lead by example.

When we undoubtedly get frustrated (remember it's like a family), it's important to learn how to control that frustration. What you do to let off steam behind closed doors doesn't affect your team like when you "lose it" in front of them. Taking a consistent and calm approach will affect the situations more positively than abrupt knee-jerk reactions that will create chaos and unrest. When things get heated, step away if you have to and revisit the situation after you have time to take it all in and process it.

Being consistent with all of our team members equally can be a challenge. Don't lie to yourself and think that by going easier on those "good" employees when they don't live up to standards is doing you or the organization any good. If you don't hold everyone to the same standards all the time in every circumstance and instance you will inadvertently alienate and distance yourself from your team.

The team sees and feels what is going on when there is tension, whether you think they know about or not. No one can keep a secret and no one does. Just stay consistent, act with honesty and integrity and you will sleep much better at night and your team will respect you more in the long run.

Trust is lost or gained by being consistent. If your team knows that when they approach you, and you are consistently level-headed and calm, they will continue to come to you. With both successes and failures, wins and losses. They trust you, they know you will be there for them regardless of what they bring to you. They will look forward to bringing successes and they won't try to hide failures. But when they don't know how you will react, or if they know that your reaction will potentially be over-the-top and emotional... They will stay away from you as long as they can-even if its good news they have for you. They will go to someone else, someone who is more consistent in their approach and reactions. It's your job to be the person they want to come to. Be the manager that your team needs and that you want to be.

Do your best to be consistent, objective and unemotional.

(Standards + Accountability) Consistency

= **Success**

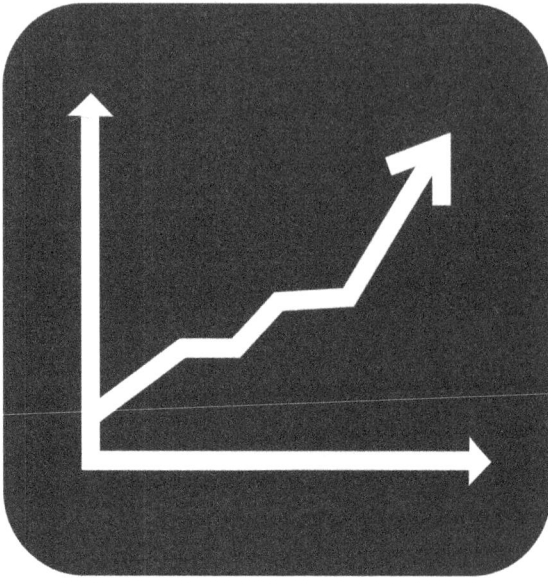

(Standards + Accountability) Consistency = **Success**

Everyone is probably going to have a different definition of success. Much of how we see success can be linked to things like accomplishing goals. In a fine dining restaurant maybe your goal is to obtain, or maintain, a one, two or three Michelin star designation. In a hotel setting maybe you would want five diamonds. In a healthcare setting maybe you want to have high retail sales along with patient satisfaction scores in the 90's. For a food truck you may want a huge following so that every time you pull up or park somewhere there is a crowd waiting for you. In a casual dining setting maybe you want five star social media reviews. Whatever segment of the industry you work in, most of us want to be good at what we do and recognized by our peers, customers, regulatory authorities or our team members as being successful.

Regardless of what we see as success, or what our goals are, it takes people to make this happen. It has been said that employees don't leave jobs they leave managers. There is some truth to that. Think back to your best job situations, where you felt most fulfilled. Chances are these were not always the highest paid positions, but they were positions that you probably learned a lot and had great relationships in. Positions that you felt valued for your contributions as a team member and/or counterpart.

Most of the time, we get too hung up over money. We think that money is the determining factor for people wanting to come work for us or for leaving us. Now, I'm not saying that it's not a factor, because it is. But if money is a factor for someone leaving us or not wanting to join our team then chances are we know about that well before someone moves on to another position or company or even takes the job initially.

Yes, for most of us, we work for money. We have to be able to make a living on what we make and if we can't then we have to look for something that will help us do that. But how many times have you seen someone go somewhere else for the same salary or for something like an additional $1 an hour?

Not life changing money, but more than they were making before. In our current food environment probably more than once. Food service is competitive and is only going to get more so. People are not clamoring to get into the hospitality industry like they are the tech industry or to become doctors and lawyers. Many people get into this industry because they don't have other options and we, as the hospitality industry, are always hiring.

We shouldn't focus on the things we can't control-they are what they are.

What we can do is try to create environments that help team members become successful. Whether they stay in the industry, move on to other jobs within the industry or whether they use the industry as a stepping stone to get into what they really want to do. I have found that the factors that predominately determine if a person stays or goes to another property or even another industry are almost always not financial in nature.

Which leads us to why understanding motivation is so important.

Chapter #6

Motivation

Think back to a time that you were truly happy and felt fulfilled in your job. Chances are it could have been any combination of things as to why you felt that way. You had a great boss, loved your coworkers, felt like you had meaningful and challenging work to do, could pay your bills on time and even and even had from time-to-time some left over after.

Or maybe it was something different. Maybe you had more time off in that job and therefore had more time to pursue your passions or hobbies. Maybe you had a flexible work schedule that allowed you to sleep in or take off early. Maybe they had a policy that you could eat whatever you wanted off the menu(s) or had "family meals" and that helped you pay your bills a little easier because you didn't have to buy much food.

Whatever the case, the key here is that everyone is motivated by different things. Those things can change over time as our life changes. As we get older our needs and desires evolve as we move into different phases of life. What motivates us when we are young, seldom motivates us as we get older. That's why how we motivate our employees needs to adapt and change also.

How to Motivate

First, you have to know <u>what </u>motivates people. Because we are motivated by different things, we have find out what motivates our team as individuals. Don't get me wrong, generalized rewards can be good for the whole team to help bring them together and have them work toward a common goal. But very few people that I know are highly motivated by pizza parties once they are out of grade school…

Second, find ways within your means to accommodate what motivates them without hurting your team. For example, say you have a server that says that they are motivated by more time off. Maybe you can find a way to have them work longer shifts when they work so that they get their hours, but can also get the time off they desire. There may be other situations where someone may just want to work part time during the week.

Aligning these two situations and letting your team member who wants more time off with the one who wants to just work part time can make a win-win-win situation for everyone. You have the coverage you need and they have the schedules they want. Rarely is it this easy, especially when you have multiple employees that have multiple needs and desires-some of which are in direct opposition to each other. But that doesn't mean you don't at least try. If you try and it doesn't work, then communicating to them and letting them know the "why" it doesn't work and not just a blanket "no" will help them understand. They might even be able to help you come up with a solution.

Third, follow up regularly with goal setting and reviews. With an environment of open communication and consistent management, you will still need to adapt to employees needs as they arise. The best way to know what needs have changed or what adaptations need to be made is by doing regular reviews. Now "regular" is relative to you and your establishment. Depending on how big your staff is, it becomes more challenging the bigger your numbers are. If it's just you and one other person, monthly or even weekly reviews could be beneficial. In big organizations that might mean monthly, quarterly, bi-annually or even annual reviews. Whatever the time frame, be sure to be consistent in your follow-up. Goal setting can be incredibly useful to keep people on track and looking toward the future. Team members look forward to their reviews (most of the time) and are more likely to follow through with goals if they are consistently followed up with. For more detail on doing this, there are probably a hundred books and ways that you can do this, so I'll refer you to those in learning how to set goals and hold people accountable to those goals. But regardless of how you set it up... Just stay consistent in your follow up.

Chapter 7

Systems vs. People

Whether we are embarking on creating a new standard for putting deliveries away or designating how long we want an order to sit in the window before it is picked up, creating systems is more important than relying on people.

Most of us might understand this, but from what I have seen, we do the exact opposite. Instead of creating a system for putting orders away, we designate people, not necessarily positions to put it away. Instead of showing and helping get food out quickly we just put our best people who get it out quickest in the position to just do it and take care of it. Now understand that I'm not necessarily opposed to this, but what happens when people call out sick, get in car accidents or surprise us by pulling the classic no-call no show?

I am a big fan of what Jim Collins in *Good to Best* refers to as "putting aces in their places." It's great to have our superstars in their key roles. But if we don't have a system for how things are done and that system is not somehow documented, and that system has multiple people knowing and understanding what it is, we are setting ourselves up for failure when people fail us.

It's a disheartening thing to think about really. But again, think about your family. There are times where we as children let our parents down, or when we as parents let our children down. No one is perfect and regardless of intent, there are times that each of us don't rise to the occasion. That's why having a system that can be followed when people don't show or go on vacation or just simply walk away for whatever reason(s), is crucial to our consistent success.

Our lives as managers and employees are made significantly easier when we have systems in place. Our rock star employees don't worry about going on vacation or taking time off because they know that their position will be covered. We as managers don't have to fret over what we are going to do to try to cover a position. Systems can create piece of mind. Systems when properly implemented and constantly updated, simply put-work.

Chapter #8

Pulling off the Band Aid

There is no substitute for hard (or difficult) work.

So, you may ask, how exactly does that apply to what we are talking about? Well, I have learned that most people aren't good at getting things done. People have a natural tendency to try to do the least amount possible. For example, if we need to have a difficult conversation with a team member, its probably not the first thing you want to do. You may instead decide to "do it after lunch" or "tomorrow."

Being a good manager isn't easy, and its never going to be. Does it get easier with practice, sure. But don't kid yourself, being a food service manager is not for someone who doesn't like:

- making decisions,
- having hard conversations or
- leading by example.

The most successful people in our industry do just that. They have hard conversations, they lead by example and they make decisions when they need to. Although we're talking specifically about the food service business, I would venture to say that these principles apply to just about any manager in any industry.

The analogy of pulling the band aid off is applicable because the faster we do some of these hard things the faster things get better-but we have to do it!

It's much easier to read another book, listen to another podcast or audio book or speech on leadership and management and tell ourselves that we need to "learn how" to do it before we take action.

Yes, if you haven't done something before it can be difficult and scary. If that's the case, get someone to mentor you and watch how they do it. The best managers generally emulate leaders that they look up to, so find a mentor and have them show you how they do it. Even if you don't formally ask someone, look at someone you respect and watch how they do things. Ask them questions as situations arise and really anytime you have a question. Good leaders recognize the need to coach and teach others, because they themselves have been coached and mentored.

Look at anyone successful, read any of their books or listen to any of their speeches or interviews and they will talk about the people that tutored them and helped them become who they are. Anyone who says they are self-made is full of it. None of us would be anywhere without guidance and mentorship from others.

But the greatest lesson that anyone can learn is to take action and fail and then continue on regardless. You will fail. You will have failures. Just don't be defined by those failures and don't let them hold you back from trying again or moving forward. Expect them to happen and expect to learn from them. Learning from failures and moving forward is the secret to failing well.

Failing is another way we rip the band aid off. It hurts, we don't want to do it. But failing is part of our change and our personal evolution. Failing leads to learning and growth.

If you're humble and communicative with your team you can lessen your failures, or at least the sting of those failures. When everyone feels that they are a part of the process and you get their feedback, then failures can be seen as failing as a team, not as individuals. Then you all learn from the mistake and move forward together. No one person is singled out and therefore no one person has to bear the brunt of the consequences of a mistake.

Be humble and do hard things. When you have to fire that employee because they need to be let go for the good of the whole organization and you have to fill in their position until you find someone new...do it! It won't last forever.

Be communicative and open to feedback. Realize you're not the smartest person in the room and that the collective knowledge of the team can in the very least provide insights into potential pitfalls of a decision that you may not have otherwise seen.

Make hard decisions and have difficult conversations sooner rather than later. Do hard things. Rip those band-aids off and move on for your own sake as well as the sake of your whole team/department/facility.

We hesitate too often to make difficult decisions for selfish reasons. We don't want to have uncomfortable conversations because we are simply uncomfortable having them. We don't want to be seen as the "bad guy" or we are afraid that someone will quit, or get mad at us or any other number of reasons. But by not having those conversations we don't always realize how the rest of our team (who recognizes there is a problem that needs to be dealt with) sees us. If we are too timid and unwilling to have a difficult conversation with a difficult employee, we are showing our team that we don't value them as much as we should. Our actions or inactions speak louder than words. Our teams see it regardless of whether or not we think they do.

We hold off on making changes that would benefit our whole department because of a few naysayers. People who are probably not going to support us in changing anything anyway. They don't want to change and so they do anything they can to delay or challenge projects. Most of the time this is simply because of ignorance. People are generally afraid of anything that they don't understand. Don't let the good of the many be dictated by the bad attitudes of the few.

Rip that band-aid off!

Conclusion

The whole point of this book can really be summed up in this…

Serve your team members as the type of leader you would want to serve. Treat your employees how you would like to be treated, communicate with them and give them what they need to be successful.

That's it.

When I set out writing this I had no agenda. In fact I really didn't even know what I was going to write, I just felt like I should start writing. I'm honestly kind of surprised at how it came together and how much I had in my head. I didn't refer to any books or studies, I simply poured out what I had in my head and my heart. I say my head and heart because I don't think they are mutually exclusive.

Even though it might not make sense in theory, it is entirely possible to manage objectively while still having empathy. You can be firm but fair, have high standards and hold people accountable while having people be so endeared to you that they cry you leave, or they leave you.

The role of a manager is that of a teacher. The kind of teacher that loves what they do and teaches with both passion and authenticity. The teacher that you go back and visit years later and thank them for the lessons that you continue to carry with you. Lessons that continually carry you forward.

I have had so many co-workers and students come back to me over the years and do just this. It truly makes my whole existence to know that I have been a source of good in this ever changing and more and more challenging world.

I spent time in kitchens and establishments where I felt belittled and afraid. I worked in places where I was afraid to look at my managers for fear of being the target of hostility. And although I wouldn't change my experiences because they have made me who I am, I would never want anyone to endure undue hardships. Especially in this sometimes thankless and incredibly discouraging business. Stereotypically speaking, food service is not for the faint of heart or the thin skinned individual. I have personally had moments in my management career that I am not proud of. Moments that I would have handled much differently had I known what I know now. With that said, by no means am I currently perfect in anything I do. I have learned that I can learn something from anyone, and anyone who says otherwise is kidding themselves.

What I do know is that regardless of what capacity, or segment of the industry we work in we can be an example of leadership and goodness. Either as a team member, a manager or whatever role we might currently occupy. We can be empathetic and caring without compromising our standards or position. It might take practice to learn how to do it, especially if we are not currently that person, but it is worth it.

Our people are worth it.

One of the greatest mentors I have ever had once told me that no one has the right to make anyone else's job harder. That is something I have carried with me ever since. It has become part of me, shaped me and influenced my decisions and how I do the things I do.

Be a mentor, be a leader, be an example of goodness and quality. Be the person that someone you tutor wants to emulate. Follow the formula…

Become a servant leader. Create standards and hold people accountable to those standards consistently and objectively. And of course, enjoy your successes and know that as you and your team work at it, you have earned it.

About the Author

Shawn Bucher MBA, CEC, CCE, CCP, CDM, CFPP

Chef Shawn has worked in almost every segment of the foodservice industry. He holds business degrees and certificates in Business, Culinary Arts, Hospitality & Tourism Management, Accounting and Professional Sales. He is a Certified Executive Chef (CEC) and a Certified Culinary Educator (CCE) through The American Culinary Federation. A Certified Culinary Professional (CCP) through the International Association of Culinary Professionals. A Certified Dietary Manager and Certified Food Protection Professional (CDM, CFPP) through the Association for Nutrition and Foodservice Professionals. He is the author of *The First Timer's Cookbook* and *The First Timer's Bakebook* and of course - *Food People Management*.

His work has been recognized nationwide as well as being a regular contributor to numerous food service publications and outlets. He is the recipient of numerous awards and just loves people.

Chef Shawn is currently a food service consultant and the owner of multiple food service businesses. To hear more from Chef Shawn, listen to the *Business Chef* Podcast.

For more information or to inquire about speaking events or other collaborative opportunities, please visit http://www.businesschef.org or email info@businesschef.org

Prologue

This was an article that I wrote back in 2015 after spending a few days in one of the most dysfunctional kitchens I had ever worked in. It was dirty, chaotic and just kind of miserable to be in. After spending time watching how people interacted and the general attitudes and demeanor of everyone, I realized that their spice rack was the perfect metaphor for the kitchen and situation itself.

The Spice Rack:
A Culinary Coach's Manifesto to Cooks Everywhere

By: Chef Shawn Bucher MBA, CEC, CCE, CCP, CDM, CFPP

You can tell a lot about a kitchen by looking at the spice rack. How clean it is, how organized or disorganized it is, if the staff is educated and trained properly or if they are just kind of winging-it. Most importantly you can tell if it is a place that you would want to eat.

Before I go into detail about this, let me introduce myself. My name is Shawn Bucher and I am a chef. I have worked in almost every food service segment that there is. I started in a grocery store meat department cleaning up after the butchers at night when I was fourteen. I did some time in independent restaurants, a big hotel, chain restaurants and franchises both on the corporate end and the franchisee end. I then got into teaching culinary school as a chef instructor, writing some cookbooks and doing some consulting. Which is what I do now for everyone from large multi-national chains to ma and pa restaurants and a lot of big and small hospitals in between. I travel a lot and I see a lot of kitchens and here are a few things I have learned over the years.

The Actual Spice Rack
The food service kitchen world is very diverse. For example, full-service restaurants are generally set-up differently than say a small grocery store deli or a big university or a hospital or hotel kitchen. They have different pieces of equipment, different layouts (usually much smaller) and different levels of food quality. Plus, employee's skill sets are very different in different kitchens.

Even with all the differences in size, food quality and staff there is a universal constant: the spice rack. There might even be numerous racks, but regardless of whether it is one or ten, without a word the spice rack tells the story of that kitchen. I'm not talking about the spice racks that look a little cluttered and messy during prime-time in a kitchen (because most of them do). I'm talking about the racks that look like this more often than not.

A Disorganized Spice Rack
This tells me that you don't take the time to organize things so that they are easily found. It tells me that you don't value other employee's time or efforts as much as you should. I can deduce that there is a lack of teamwork and cohesion in your kitchen.

It also tells me that your food cost is not as accurate as it could be because there is no way that you know everything that is on there-and when you can't find something, instead of digging through the mess of clutter you just go grab another one from the storeroom and stack it on the rack with everything else.

This behavior in-and-of itself tells me that you're always in too much of a hurry to really take time and pride in what you do. Because of this your food is probably not presented, garnished or even cooked as well as it could be.

Dirty Containers and Miss-labeled Spices
This lets me know that you don't value your ingredients and that you probably don't know how those ingredients even got there.

I used to make sure that all my cooks knew what went into getting those particular herbs and spices in those bottles. Once you understand some of the sacrifice that goes into getting certain herbs and spices into those convenient little containers, and the absolute dedication exhibited by people who are generally paid very little to do the necessary back-breaking labor (that most of us shy away from) to get all those little peppercorns or saffron crocuses into that nice container, you learn to appreciate each one of those tiny particles much more and are not so fast to just discard the leftovers or extra ingredients.

The fact that these containers are now crusted in whatever was on your hands recently (or not so recently depending on how petrified the crust is on the bottle) shows me you don't value sanitation as much as you should. It tells me that I may be taking my life in my own hands if I dare to sit down and eat whatever those hands have thrown together that day.

Everything that could possibly fit is on the Rack
I see laziness and selfishness. You don't want to take the extra steps to store it right because it is inconvenient for you. You see your time as more important that everyone else's.

As a result of seeing this I now know that you don't discard the parchment paper when you cook off items like bacon in the oven before taking the pans to the dish room. You don't scrape or dump or discard extra little bits of un-usable food before taking pots and pans to the dish room. You care about saving money for your employer and so you don't take the extra time to use a spatula to get the last portion of sauce, soup or dressing out of the container.

One of the most remarkable culinarians I have ever worked with lives by the motto, "no one has the right to make someone else's job harder." This is something I have embraced and stand firmly behind. We are all on the same team, let's act like it. This business is hard enough as it is, don't make it any harder or cause someone else any more work than you have to.

A Dirty Storage Rack
Dust and grease build-up, spilled herbs and spices, sticky dirty shelves. . . This shows me your kitchen never really gets clean. You might wipe things down here and there, and you might actually use the properly diluted sanitize solution. But when was the last time you got on your hands and knees and scrubbed with soap and hot water? When was the last time you caught all of the corners and crevasses, the walls and the condensers, the legs and undersides of the tables, the inside of the ice machines and the top and sides of the ovens, griddles and fryers? As I look around I can confidently say that it hasn't been recently.

Bent Pans and Broken Containers
I'll bet that you don't think you have enough equipment or the right equipment to get the job done. You don't value what you do have because you don't take care of it. You throw pots and pans in the sinks and drop them on the floors and throw things out if they look like they are too hard or too time

consuming to clean. You don't take responsibility for your actions and you point fingers instead of manning up, taking the heat, learning from it and improving. If you burn something, you just throw it in the dish room so that someone else has to take care of it.

I would also wager to say that there is no formal training program to help you move forward, take on more responsibility and make more money. Maybe no one has ever showed you how to take care of your equipment. I'm sure there is not a schedule to get things consistently clean or if there is it is not followed. There is little to no accountability for your actions when things get damaged. No one holds your feet to the fire if something is amiss and your superiors find it is easier to "deal with later," which might as well translate to never.

The Good News

The good news to all of this is that you can change all of this right now. You can be the change that you want. You can rise to the occasion and you can start anew. You can care enough to do things right. You can take the time to clean, to organize and to be an example of what you know you can and should be. You can take pride in what you do and you can become whatever you want to become.

What will make you successful is not the first time you clean it, but longer you consistently maintain it. The longer you maintain it, the more you have changed for the better. Your kitchen is progressively cleaner, people are happier and more willing to help each other and you will actually look forward to going to work.

It all starts by cleaning your spice rack.

www.ingramcontent.com/pod-product-compliance
Lightning Source LLC
Chambersburg PA
CBHW031417180326
41458CB00002B/414

9 780578 507095